P.

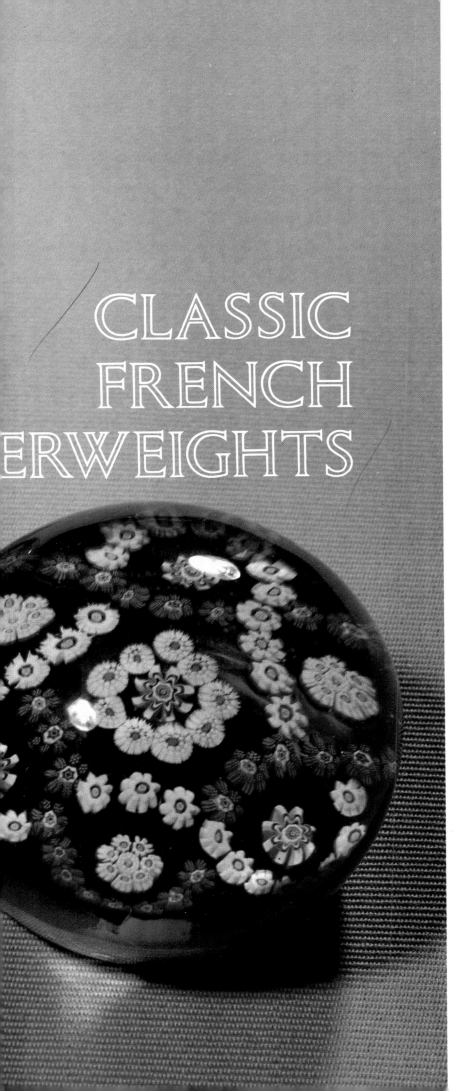

CLASSIC
FRENCH
[PAP]ERWEIGHTS

by Edith Mannoni

Edited by
Paul Jokelson
and
Lawrence H. Selman

PAPERWEIGHT PRESS
SANTA CRUZ, CALIFORNIA

< *Frontispiece:*

Seen from above, a close packed millefiori, encircled by a
white filigreed ring in a red torsade. In profile, it looks like an
upright, mushroom-shaped tuft. One notes red and green trefoils and many stars, characteristic of Baccarat, the only maker
to achieve spaced upright canes, which are always in concentric
rows in Saint Louis. $3\frac{1}{4}''$ in diameter, $2''$ high. Suger collection.

< *Title page:*

On the right, two garlands, one white, the other blue, entwined
over a garnet ground. On the left, a more subtle pattern of five
chains, each encircling a floret, one of which is a pink rose.
Above, concentric millefiori, one of which is made up of
twelve tiny roses. All are Clichy. Dary collection.

Translated from the French by Karen Kay
Designed by Linda Marcetti
Set in Monophoto Apollo

Library of Congress Cataloging in Publication Data
Mannoni, Edith.
    Classic French paperweights.

    Translation of: Les Sulfures et boules presse-papiers.
    1. Sulphides (Art)—France—History—19th century.
2. Paperweights—France—History—19th century.
I. Jokelson, Paul, 1905–   II. Selman, Lawrence.
III. Title.
NK5540.S8M3613   1984   748.8'4'0944   84-61013
ISBN 0-933756-06-2

CLASSIC FRENCH PAPERWEIGHTS

ORIGINS

In eighteenth-century Europe, competition was keen among the great glass producers: Venice, Bohemia, England and France. Venice lost its lead but still enjoyed a monopoly over certain traditions, those of rather special designs, filigree adornments and so-called milk-white, opaque glass threads. Bohemia was famous for the quality and the unique coloring of its crystal. As for the English—they invented crystal!

This was what first provoked French rivalry to such a great degree. "There is no country where the English have not managed to introduce their crystal and glassware," moaned a report by the Académie des Sciences in 1771. "In the past, they took almost all the glass they needed from France. Today, they supply us with chandeliers, lanterns, drinking glasses."

France actively sought to catch up with its competitors. Two glassworks, destined to a great future, were created: in 1764, Sainte Anne in Baccarat and in 1767, Saint Louis, near Bitche, both in Lorraine, whose rich forests provided wood for fuel.

French efforts were to meet with tremendous success. Their crystal was to enjoy an unequalled flourishing during the first half of the nineteenth century and was to be used to produce many different objects of exceptional beauty. Thus France surpassed its rivals and succeeded in mastering all their techniques.

< This jelly dish is a good illustration of a certain Saint Louis style of various objects on paperweight bases. Also very typical of Saint Louis is the white latticinio or filigree spiral bowl and the cover's rim adorned with a torsade in red. The base is a common Saint Louis pattern. Musée des Cristalleries de Saint Louis in Paris.

SULPHIDES

The art of making ceramic inclusions in crystal was discovered in France in 1780 by M. de Beaufort, director of Saint Louis from 1775 to 1788. Between 1779 and 1782, Boyer and Philippe-Charles Lambert learned manufacturing secrets from a Bohemian glassmaker, Joseph Koenig, a defector from an English glassworks. They founded a glassworks in Sèvres in 1783 under the patronage of Marie-Antoinette. In 1785 this business was transferred to Montcenis, near Creusot, close to abundant deposits of coal, which at that time was a new source of fuel.

This factory, called the Queen's, Montcenis', or Creusot's, was to become famous under the Empire and the Restoration for the quality of its crystal. It is credited with some exceptional sulphides.

Cameos were brought into fashion by the return to antiquity triggered by the Pompeii and Herculaneum discoveries (1750). They were made of finely molded clay. Wedgwood of England became their champion. An attempt was made to cover them with crystal in order to lend them more brilliancy and to enlarge the image. The high temperature of the molten crystal, however, deteriorated them; the cameo adhered poorly and air bubbles formed. Henri-Germain Boileau succeeded, however, in making sulphides as early as 1790. The museum of the Conservatoire des Arts et Métiers has two of his creations dated 1798 with cameos of Voltaire and Franklin.

An adventurous soul, Chevalier Pierre Honoré Boudon de Saint Amans, seems to have perfected the

These glass earrings recall the first known paperweight (1845) made by the Venetian Pietro Bigaglia. Each contains various fragments of colored glass and a pink and white cane containing the silhouette of a gondola in the center. One can discern segments of aventurine with its reddish-brown, metallic reflections, also found in Murano paperweights. The settings date these objects between 1830 and 1840. Private collection.

technique. Born in 1774, he managed to escape the courts of the Terror. He was forced to join the armies which were to land in England and was taken prisoner. He took advantage of his stay in England to refine his knowledge of clay. Back in France during the Restoration, he registered a patent in 1818 for "the manufacture of portraits, in the cameo style, encased in crystal with color added."

The glass factory at Creusot bought and worked this patent. The cameo was based on kaolin mixed with potassium silicate, so that it would have the same density as the crystal, in order to bear its weight without damage. Later, steatite was used; this is a hydrated silicate of magnesium or "French chalk." Upon contact with crystal, the cameo took on a metallic luster similar to that of silver sulphide, hence the name "sulphide" for these objects.

In 1800 a M. Paris, "jeweler and manufacturer of orders of the cross," opened a shop near the Palais-Royal at 13, rue Croix-des-Petits-Champs. He specialized in the inclusion in crystal of enameled subjects of various colors, often on gold, such as decorations, flowers or figurines. His success was such that he founded the Bercy glassworks in 1828 to satisfy the demand.

He did not restrict himself to decorating pendants, trinkets or plaques in this manner. He also ornamented sulphides, the enameled subjects of case and box covers, and stoppers, sides and bottoms of glass decanters. Later Baccarat was to draw inspiration from these creations for various objects such as paperweights, primarily for a rare and highly prized example called Legion of Honor.

These techniques, however, were relatively simple. Many ceramists, artisans and glass-cutters in France, Bohemia and Great Britain produced sulphides.

On the other hand, beautiful paperweights required delicate and complex manufacturing techniques in which three French factories were to excel: Baccarat, Saint Louis and Clichy. They would be imitated in France itself, as well as in England, the United States and Bohemia. This interesting period was to be brief,

Clear crystal footed bowl decorated with thin slices of millefiori canes. Baccarat. Private collection.

Small candy dish in cut crystal with a sulphide on a gold leaf base in the middle of the cover. It bears a cameo of Louis XVIII. Baccarat. Halphen-Meyer collection.

On the left, a typical Baccarat weight with millefiori canes in vivid hues sprinkled on an upset muslin ground. Two of them, one yellow and one blue, bear silhouettes which are unique to Baccarat (here, a rooster and a deer). In the center, a newel post with canes suspended in crystal. At the right, one of the most treasured Baccarat patterns, a butterfly on an upset muslin ground surrounded by millefiori. The wings are also millefiori. Private collection.

although its end is not truly known (about 1860?). However, its beginning undoubtedly occurred around the year 1845.

In spite of many detailed historical studies by various experts from that time on, it is not known how a European of the 1840s got the idea of including millefiori and other fantasies inside a flat-bottomed ball of glass for use as a paperweight. Although transparent, these impressive objects conceal many secrets. The millefiori embedded in them take us back to the pale dawn of civilization.

MILLEFIORI

The Italian word *millefiori* (a thousand flowers) was coined in 1836 by Heinrich von Minutoli, a German. It conjures up the image of a field sprinkled with flowers and of a design created from multicolored and extraordinarily arranged slices of glass canes.

Creating millefiori canes is a technical *tour de force*. In order to make one, the glassblower gathers a small mass of molten glass or crystal onto the end of his blowpipe from a "pot" in an oven. He rolls his gather on a marble slab (marver) in order to shape it into a cylindrical form. This roll is dipped into a pot containing molten glass or crystal of another color and the blower then rolls this into a cylinder. In this manner he is able to add different layers of color, forming a rather thick cylinder up to two inches in diameter. When the millefiori is finished, he reheats it and has an assistant pull the free end of the cylinder with a pontil (an iron rod). The assistant pulls away quickly. The hot glass column is drawn out until it is something less than half an inch in thickness. The cane is then cut into segments. These slices show concentric circles of the colors used to make the cane.

With molds, various designs besides circles can be made. A hot cane is pressed into a grooved cylinder, resulting in a more or less closely folded serration of

[5]

Detail of a Baccarat weight with canes on a muslin ground. In it, we can see numerous figurines (elephant, horse, rooster, deer, butterfly) as well as the date signature cane *B 1848*. Halphen-Meyer collection.

The first French crystal paperweights were close packed mille-fiori, a dense composition of various canes, gathered as if at random, like wild flowers of the field scattered by the wind. Here are two examples from Baccarat: on the left, a miniature paperweight, 2″ in diameter; on the right, a 3½″ magnum. The latter contains canes with animal silhouettes and the date *1848*. Boisgirard.

This enlargement of a Baccarat weight reveals, among other things, the silhouette of a hunter in a cane with a serrated green exterior. Halphen-Meyer collection.

The millefiori may be arranged in a concentric pattern. These three weights illustrate three different paperweight sizes. In the middle, a signed and dated Saint Louis weight of the most common diameter, approximately 2½″, between two Baccarat weights, one miniature, about 2″, and a magnum approximately 3⅛″. Boisgirard.

This view of a close packed millefiori allows us to see the variety of the florets within it. It is dated *1847* and signed *B* (for Baccarat). When present the *B* is located above the two middle digits, between the *8* and the *4*. Clean, fresh colors. Halphen-Meyer collection.

Miniature weight showing a very typical Baccarat design: nine canes with red exteriors are decorated with tiny blue arrows pointed at a red, six-sided star placed in the center. This view gives us some idea of the lovely play between light and transparency due to the position of canes sandwiched between two layers of beautiful crystal. 2″ in diameter. Boisgirard.

This incredibly detailed millefiori contains 233 different canes, eight with silhouettes: a deer, three dogs, a rooster, two roses, a butterfly and, above all, an exceptional date, *1853*. Dates on Baccarat weights usually range from 1846 to 1849 inclusive. This one was found in the foundation of the church built in 1853 at Baccarat. Musée de Baccarat in Paris.

Beautiful concentric millefiori suspended over a translucent amber ground. Seven red arrows turn toward the center, encircled by twelve white stars marked with red dots. 3⅛" in diameter, 2" high. Baccarat. Suger collection.

Over a translucent red ground, six circles of millefiori around a large central floret with a complex central cane. Three circles of white and salmon pink canes with a star marked with red at the center and three other circles of white and red florets with serrated green exteriors. In the middle, canes composed of white stars and a center of little green circles, around tiny blue arrows pointed at a star marked with red. Baccarat. 3⅛" in diameter, 2" high. Suger collection.

the slice. The central cane is placed, when hot, into a star or trefoil mold, or into an assortment of other shapes. A wealth of combinations is possible by using various molds and colors.

This delicate technique seems to date back to antiquity. Ancient Egypt left millefiori mosaics from the eighteenth dynasty of the New Empire (approximately 1580 B.C.). Glass rods with miniaturized motifs appeared as ornaments on vases of the fifteenth century B.C. found in Mesopotamia.

During the first centuries B.C. and A.D. Rome and the Middle East were producing quantities of glass bowls with millefiori designs. In Greece, at Kenchreai, several mosaics from the fourth century A.D. made with filigree appeared in Venice in the middle of the sixteenth century. During the seventeenth and eighteenth centuries Murano glassmakers enclosed mille-Mediterranean region or to Greco-Roman civilization.

The Venetians either inherited or rediscovered this technique. In 1494 a Venetian writer named Sabellico (in his study of the Murano glass industry) evoked the person "to whom it first occurred to include in a little ball all the sorts of flowers which clothe the meadows in spring." He is probably referring to the small glass spheres in which slices of millefiori had

been enclosed. Some of them, pierced with a hole, were supposed to be worn on chains as jewelry.

One of these balls in a private collection is about two inches in diameter. It contains a tiny milk-white glass plaque bearing the portrait of a young man done in the style of Carpaccio, surrounded by millefiori florets. It dates back to the sixteenth century. Some were probably known earlier, however; in his catalogue, Duc Jean de Berry (1340–1416) cites decorated *pommes de voirre* (apples of glass).

A catalogue (1495) from the Giovanni Barovier factory in Murano mentions dagger hilts containing millefiori. Bowls, flasks and ewers from Venice were also decorated with millefiori. Two exquisite ewers of this type which belonged to Henry VIII (1491–1547) are on exhibit at the British Museum. Vases decorated with filigree appeared in Venice in the middle of the sixteenth century. During the seventeenth and eighteenth centuries Murano glassmakers enclosed millefiori and filigree in silverware handles and also in decorative columns, such as the seventeen-inch high column on display at the British Museum.

Close packed millefiori upright mushroom with the base encircled by a blue and white torsade. Green stars appear amid red trefoils and a myriad of red, white and blue stars. $3\frac{1}{8}''$ in diameter, $2\frac{1}{8}''$ high. Baccarat. Suger collection.

Two references reveal that decorated balls and millefiori were known in eighteenth-century France. In 1756, the extremely erudite priest Jean-Jacques Barthélémy (1716–1795) wrote to the Comte de Caylus, an archaeology enthusiast, about how happy he was to own a small pale yellow glass sphere decorated with enameled bouquets. It was probably one of the Venetian balls of the Renaissance, which were often yellow.

This same Caylus, in his monumental *Recueil d'antiquités égyptiennes, étrusques, grecques, romaines et gauloises* (Study of Egyptian, Etruscan, Greek, Roman and Gallic antiquities) (1752–1767) described the production of millefiori mosaics in a way which demonstrates a perfect understanding of the process.

It seems that millefiori also began to surface in northern Europe; in 1786 a German named Bruckmann rediscovered the technique. Copies of Roman millefiori bowls seem to have been made near the beginning of the nineteenth century. This assertion is made based on the collection of the English archaeologist Dodwell (1767–1832) now in the sculpture museum in Munich. In 1833 another German, W. E. Foss, succeeded in making millefiori and exhibited them in Mainz in 1842. The Zenker works in Bohemia seems to have followed

Upright mushroom of concentric millefiori in a double overlay weight—turquoise on white. It is cut with seven round windows and a star-cut base. At the center, a red star marked with a blue dot is surrounded by nine tiny arrows. $3\frac{1}{8}''$ in diameter, $2\frac{3}{8}''$ high. Baccarat. Suger collection.

Two views of a white clematis with ten veined petals. At the center, eight tiny green arrows turn toward a red star marked with a blue dot. Five green leaves. Six round windows are cut on the sides and one larger one at the top. The base is star cut. Baccarat. Boisgirard.

On the left, a blue and white primrose. At its heart, twenty-three white stars and a red center. Five leaves around the flower, plus two branches with five leaves at the stem.

On the right, a white clematis with twelve veined petals. A star at the center, surrounded by tiny arrows and stars. Six leaves frame the flower. The stem bears three leaves and a bud. A circle of millefiori on the periphery. Cut with seven facets and a star-cut base. Baccarat.

At the top, a sulphide with a cameo of Empress Marie-Louise marked with an *A* on the back, probably referring to Bertrand Andrieu, one of the great sulphide makers. Possibly made by Creusot. Darys collection.

Friedrich Egermann's recipe (1837) for color combinations in mosaics and millefiori. Flasks, buttons and jewelry decorated with millefiori were produced in the Jablonz region north of Bohemia.

SUCCESSFUL REDISCOVERY

During this time, France made up for its lag with quite a flourish; crystal production reached a very high level. Techniques for including cameos or enameled subjects in crystal were completely mastered. Magnifi-

cent opalines proved that the French had a remarkable talent for coloring crystal, and this provoked quite a reaction on the part of Bohemian glassmakers.

In order to undercut French pre-eminence, the Bohemians attempted to make their colored glass even more spectacular and more affordable. They were successful; they flooded the French market.

This was a time of profound economic and social change in Europe. With the revolutions of 1839, an elegant and demanding clientele witnessed the diminishing of its resources as a larger and upwardly mobile

[11]

middle class began to appear—a class interested in less expensive *objets d'art*. French crystal makers attempted to adjust to this development and to compete with Bohemian glassmakers. One of their strategies was to replace refined opalines with less costly articles similar to those from Bohemia. In order to do so, they had to find other coloring processes and other techniques.

The profession was restructured. In 1822, the Sainte Anne glassworks became the Baccarat crystal works on an industrial scale. Further, in 1829, the Saint Louis glassworks was transformed into the Compagnie des Verreries et Cristalleries de Saint Louis. It abandoned production of functional objects such as plate glass and branched out into the making of Bohemian glass and crystal.

The two firms came to an agreement and together they purchased the Creusot crystal works in 1832, then shut down its ovens, thus eliminating a formidable competitor in high quality crystal.

In 1835, a group of directors from various glass companies went on a research trip through Germany, Austria and Bohemia, with particular emphasis on Bohemia. That same year and in 1836, Brongniart (director of the Sèvres factory) also visited Germany, concentrating on Bohemia. He exhibited the objects brought back from this trip, some of them glass, at the ceramics museum. He even offered some of them to French glassmakers as study samples.

Also in 1836 the Société d'Encouragement pour l'Industrie Française (Society for the Promotion of French Industry) created a prize for those who could unveil the secrets of "the manufacture of hollow glass, colored or decorated in the Bohemian style." The assistant director at Baccarat, François de Fontenay, won one of these prizes in 1838, totalling 3,000 francs.

In 1837 Rouyer and Maës created a new establishment at Boulogne-sur-Seine, near the Pont de Sèvres. It was transferred to Clichy in 1844 and became the renowned Clichy works, made famous by the paperweights it was soon to manufacture. It produced a special material, a barium oxide glass, similar to crystal but much lighter. It was already well-known because of the coloring in solid tones of its vases, flasks and various other opaline curios in vogue at the time.

Some articles were done in overlay; this refers to a thin layer of glass on the surface. The overlay consists of a white opaque layer of crystal, either alone or lined with a second colored layer of the same material placed on a crystal form. The object thus covered is then cut so that the clear crystal below, lined with white or bordered by a white thread beneath the layer of color will appear.

We know that in 1839 Emile Godard, the director of Baccarat, began making double and even triple overlay crystal. However, the Saint Louis crystal works seems to have been the first to produce them.

An admirable floral composition: a twelve-petalled clematis, its center a red star, surrounded by eight tiny blue arrows and thirteen white stars with red centers. Seven leaves frame the flower. At the stem, on one side, a group of three leaves and on the other, a group of five leaves with a bud. 3″ in diameter. Baccarat. Suger collection.

This factory had already caused a stir at the 1839 Exhibit of French Industry Products (which took place every five years) with its colored crystal and at the 1844 exhibit with its "fantasy crystal of all kinds" including overlays—a technique in which it was to become a virtuoso.

Overlay paperweights are among the most valued. The example which has commanded the highest price is a blue and white Saint Louis overlay which drew $117,600 in the fever of bidding in London in 1979.

During this same period of time, other techniques were perfected or rediscovered. In 1838 a remarkable specialist, Georges Bontemps—director of the Choisy-le-Roi works (established in 1821) from 1828 to 1849—taught his workers to draw out hot crystal into very fine threads, or filigree. Even Venice, at the end of the eighteenth century, seems to have lost the secret of this technique. At the 1839 exhibit Bontemps showed some filigree vases which were still somewhat clumsy. At the 1844 show, however, perfectly mastered filigree designs from Choisy-le-Roi appeared. And Bontemps presented millefiori vases as well!

In perfecting these designs and colorings, French factories also learned how to produce less expensive

This twelve-petalled clematis is presented here in a carefully-balanced composition with its six symmetrical leaves and the two buds about to open. The stems also criss-cross in a regular pattern. The center is made of a red whorl with twenty minuscule white stars. $1\frac{3}{4}''$ in diameter, $1\frac{3}{4}''$ high. Baccarat. Suger collection.

Companion to the preceding weight. According to the same principle of composition, a red clematis with twelve narrower petals. Same center. Three leaves placed symmetrically behind the flower. The two buds are less open. Star-cut at the base. Same dimensions—$1\frac{3}{4}''$ in diameter, $1\frac{3}{4}''$ high. Baccarat. Suger collection.

items by using industrial methods and chemical processes which made manufacture quicker, easier, and less costly.

We do not know exactly why three French factories began making paperweights in 1845.

THE FIRST PAPERWEIGHTS

The idea came from Venice by way of Vienna. At the time, Venice was part of the Austrian Empire.

"Everything can be copied. The French have reproduced all the colors which had previously been the domain of the Bohemian glassmakers, and they in turn copy the French, doubling and tripling their glass production, not to mention Saint Louis, the initiator of this kind of manufacture," remarked Eugène Péligot, a professor at the Conservatoire des Arts et Métiers, in 1845. He was sent to Vienna by the Paris Chamber of Commerce to report on the Exhibition of the Products of Austrian Industry. He noted that the glassmaking display was extensive and that Venice and Bohemia were well represented. He also mentioned seeing paper-

weights presented by Pietro Bigaglia of Venice. He called them "millefiori paperweights" and went on to describe them. They were "round in shape and made of very transparent glass in which a number of small tubes of various colors and forms are gathered, producing the effect of a multitude of flowers."

It would seem that French factories awaited this revelation to launch their own paperweights. There is a large close packed millefiori which is signed and dated *SL 1845* (Saint Louis). And the factory's museum has a flask mounted on this type of base with the same signature and date. It is assumed that Péligot advised the Saint Louis factory upon his return from Vienna and they immediately began making paperweights.

It would not be the first for very long. An American museum, the Illinois State Museum in Springfield, has a Clichy paperweight mounted on a metal base with the inscription *Escalier de Cristal, 1845*. The Escalier de Cristal was a famous Palais-Royal boutique specializing in luxury items.

On March 9, 1968 the Republic of Egypt commissioned Sotheby's to compile a sales catalogue for King Farouk's valuable paperweight collection. On January 27, 1969 about 350 were put up for auction. One of

A flower repeats the colors of the two preceding weights; a rare clematis with twelve petals—six red and six longer white ones, superimposed rather than alternating. The center is a green whorl surrounded by twenty-one white stars. A fan of seven leaves behind the flower and two groups of three leaves at the stem. $2\frac{1}{2}''$ in diameter, $1\frac{5}{8}''$ high. Baccarat. Suger collection.

The famous Baccarat pansy was so popular that it was manufactured until 1907. In its most classic form, it is composed of two large violet petals and three small ones striped with yellow, each with a brown spot on the outer border. Seven leaves and one bud. The center is made up of a small pink whorl surrounded by two circles of delicate white stars. $2\frac{3}{4}''$ in diameter, $2''$ high. Halphen-Meyer collection.

them, a millefiori, bears an important mark: *B 1845*. Until that time, the earliest known Baccarat weights were dated 1846.

The French, therefore, had quickly made the transition from doing filigree to doing millefiori, where similar techniques are used. All that remained was the inclusion of florets in a crystal ball, just as cameos and enameled figurines were.

To do this, the florets were placed on an open mold plate with as many cavities as florets to be included in the paperweights. A hot gather of clear crystal was applied to the mold and then quickly removed. The side opposite the florets was flattened to form the base of the object. Then more crystal was poured over the florets and rounded out with a wet hollow wooden paddle; this was the top. The piece was then annealed, polished, and possibly cut at the wheel.

The florets quite often appear against muslin grounds, swirl latticinio and filigree lace arrangements. For this, opaque crystal threads, white or colored, or thin canes of spiral filigree were placed in molds according to the selected design. The glassmaker then took a gather of molten crystal on his blowpipe and blew it and placed this bubble on the filled mold. The threads would adhere to the surface on contact. Then the worker would inhale the air contained in the bubble, which then flattened out, forming a convex or concave cushion in which bits of filigree lay embedded.

Venice seems to have been aware of all these techniques. French paperweights, however, immediately demonstrated clear superiority over Venetian weights of the same date. The mastery shown in French work from the very first attempts is surprising.

Bohemian glassmakers tried to equal them. They apparently had to wait until 1848; this is the earliest date noted on Bohemian paperweights. Furthermore, their beautifully white and clear lime potash glass was not as clear as French crystal. The Bohemians did succeed in flooding the British market with their paperweights. The English in turn responded to this success by manufacturing their own paperweights.

The first factory to do so was Whitefriars in London, followed by two others in Birmingham—Bacchus and Islington (1848–1849). However, neither Bohemian products nor those from England were really able to rival those of France.

The three French factories, on the other hand, began a close rivalry. We have learned this from letters exchanged from 1847 to 1851 between Saint Louis and

Blue, yellow and mauve pansy in a paperweight cut with seven round windows. Star at the center, encircled by green florets with tiny arrows. Six leaves and one bud. A garland of canes with the dominant color alternating between white and green. Relief star cut extending over the entire base. $3\frac{1}{4}''$ in diameter. Baccarat. Boisgirard.

Blue camomile or pompon, its center made of yellow stamens and two circles of white stars. A branch bearing six leaves, one detached, and a red bud. Concave round window at the top. Star-cut base. $2\frac{1}{2}''$ in diameter. Baccarat. Boisgirard.

Flower weights are among those most prized. Here are four representative weights. Boisgirard.

Top left: Saint Louis camomile.

Top right: a mauve clematis with ten petals and honeycomb center. Six leaves frame it. At the stem, three leaves and a bud. A circle of canes on the outer rim and star-cut base. 3'' in diameter. Baccarat.

Bottom left: primrose from Baccarat in vermilion and white. A red whorl and two rows of little stars at the center. Five leaves behind the flower and stem with two three-leaf bouquets. $2\frac{7}{8}''$ in diameter.

Bottom right: a pink dahlia from Saint Louis. $2\frac{3}{4}''$ in diameter.

its Parisian distributor Launay, Hautin et Cie., 50, rue Paradis-Poissonière (today rue de Paradis); this correspondence was preserved in the factory's files. A letter dated December 22, 1847 and addressed to the director of Saint Louis announced that Baccarat had again improved its paperweight manufacture and was selling substantial quantities. Another letter complained that the quality of a shipment of Saint Louis paperweights was unsatisfactory and added that since Saint Louis had lost the sale, Clichy was benefiting and "cannot fulfill all the orders received."

The Revolution of 1848, aggravated by poor harvests, threatened the prosperity of all glassworks. Some, such as Choisy-le-Roi, had to close. Elsewhere, the sale of expensive items such as dinner services, candelabras and large vases was stopped. On the other hand, the tide seemed to turn in favor of paperweights, "trinkets which remained affordable in spite of everything and were still a novelty to the public." Saint Louis correspondents encouraged the production of paperweights.

At this time, red, white and blue designs glorifying the Revolution began to appear in paperweights. "These three colors pleased the glassworker who, in making a weight, expressed in this way his faith in a better future; they pleased the middle-class man who was happy to declare his liberal and republican ideas. . . . Paris, the capital of fashion, used the Revolution as a pretext for launching these trinkets which were both patriotic and Parisian." (*Les Presse-Papiers Français de Cristal* by Y. Amic and R. Imbert).

Was 1849 the year that flower weights first appeared? A letter from Launay on December 5 tells us that Baccarat brought out examples with "pansies and

A delightful example: two bellflowers and five tiny narcissus in this weight, cut with seven round windows and a large star at the base. $2\frac{3}{4}''$ in diameter. Baccarat. Private collection.

[15]

A more subtly harmonious and slightly whimsical arrangement of a white clematis with twelve petals accompanied by a small red clematis with five petals—each with honeycomb centers. Four leaves around the large flower, arranged in slightly staggered symmetry. Two leaves at the stem. A circle of millefiori on the periphery, white and red alternating with florets of red arrows with blue exteriors and white arrows with green exteriors, pointed toward red stars marked with blue dots. Clear star-cut base. $3\frac{1}{8}$" in diameter, 2" high. Baccarat. Suger collection.

various bouquets which sold well" and were less expensive than those of Saint Louis. However, flowers and tricolor bouquets seem to have been made during the revolutionary years.

Curiously, the flowers created later were easier to make than the millefiori. They were modeled and assembled when hot with pincers and shears. The same process was used for similar motifs such as fruit, butterflies and flat bouquets. Péligot's work *Le Verre, son Histoire, sa Fabrication* (Masson, 1877) describes the process; little bits of colored glass were heated red-hot "on an earthen plate to soften their angles; then they are sorted into the various cavities of a thick, open mold plate. By applying a gather of ordinary crystal to the mold and then removing it right away, all the tiny pieces of glass adhere to the gather. The piece is marvered and flattened; with the puntied base on the bottom, enough crystal to cover the base and form the weight is poured over its surface.''

The flat bouquet must be differentiated from the upright bouquet. The upright bouquet is made up of tiny flowers or millefiori florets forming a mushroom. The upright bouquet is set head first in a convex mold into which molten crystal is poured through a funnel. When it has cooled down, the block of crystal containing the motif is removed from the mold. It forms the base of the piece upon which crystal is poured to mold the top.

In April 1851 Baccarat placed ninety-five pieces in the Conservatoire des Arts et Métiers, according to the collections catalogue of the Conservatoire, thus allowing us to determine dates with some accuracy. Among these were eleven paperweights—four of them sulphides, three millefiori, four with flowers, bouquets, and a butterfly.

That same year, the Great Exhibition of the Industry of All Nations took place at the Crystal Palace in London. Clichy was the only French manufacturer present with an exhibit of its paperweights. Once again Eugene Péligot was delegated to make a report on this

Very beautifully colored pansy in deep violet and yellow with honeycomb center. Nine leaves and a bud. Surrounded by white canes with green centers and red canes encircling a blue star. Cut with five side facets and a star at the base. $2\frac{3}{8}''$ in diameter, 2″ high. Baccarat. Suger collection.

Butterfly with blue eyes and antennae, black head and purple body. Marbled wings made up of slightly flattened millefiori. Lively muslin ground decorated by a ring of green and white canes. $2\frac{7}{8}''$ in diameter. Baccarat. Suger collection.

Butterflies flying over a flower are among the most precious Baccarat weights. Here, the traditional butterfly with turquoise eyes and antennae hovers over a clematis with ten petals and a center made up of a large eight-pointed star with a smaller star of stamens at the center. Five leaves radiate from the flower. At the stem, a bud and three leaves. Star-cut base. Note the latticinio body encased in translucent amethyst. $3\frac{1}{8}''$ in diameter, $2\frac{3}{8}''$ high. Suger collection.

event for the French Commission. He admired the remarkable qualities of the Clichy weights, their pink and turquoise overlays, their muslin grounds, their filigree and their millefiori arranged in the most varied designs. Three specific Clichy millefiori weights were included in this exhibition. One was a large spaced millefiori with a crown and the initials *V* and *A*—for Queen Victoria and Prince Albert—and the legend *Londres 1851* engraved at the base. The second was a sulphide with purple ground and the inscription *Hyde Park, London 1851*. The third was a perfume flask shown in *The Illustrated Exhibitor,* a magazine devoted to the Great Exhibition. Clichy weights enchanted so many visitors that British industrialists tried to entice glassmakers away from the firm.

In 1853 Clichy was once again the only manufacturer to appear at the exhibition at the Crystal Palace in New York. Once again its paperweights stood out because of their extraordinary variety.

A deep blue flower made up of five heart-shaped petals. At the center, a pink bull's eye cane surrounded by two rows of tiny stars. Five spear-shaped leaves. Fourteen facet cuts on the sides and star cut on the base. $2\frac{1}{8}$″ in diameter, $1\frac{1}{2}$″ high. Baccarat. Suger collection.

PAPERWEIGHTS IN DECLINE

The United States slowly began to produce paperweights, first at the New England Glass Company and the Boston and Sandwich Glass Company in 1852. Most of these weights were made by workers who had come from English, French or Venetian factories.

Inspiration was drawn from certain successful French weights, such as the clematis and buttercup weights from Baccarat, Saint Louis jasper grounds and latticinio from Saint Louis and Clichy. As far as we can tell, American production lasted until about 1880.

The end of French production is not so clear. M. Launay's last letters in 1851 no longer refer to paperweights. From 1855 on, there were hardly any exhibition catalogues or other documents mentioning paperweights. Baccarat had displayed a great range of its paperweights at the Exhibition of French Industry Products in 1849 and presented a similar selection at the International Exhibition of 1855 in Paris. Prices were quite reasonable even for the snake weights (ten francs); today, these items fetch extremely high prices.

At Christie's of London on June 25, 1982 records were broken by two green snake weights: £2,592 for one and £2,808 for the second weight which was better centered. This price was higher than that obtained for a superb concentric millefiori from Clichy (£2,376) which was really a more beautiful and impressive paperweight.

A large close packed millefiori from Baccarat dated 1853 was the subject of an extraordinary adventure. When the chapel of Sainte Anne, which had been built in the courtyard of the factory in 1776, turned out to be too small in light of the growth of the business, the decision was made in 1853 to build a larger one. A lead casket containing pieces of gold and silver, two medals and an impressive paperweight made up of 233 different millefiori was sealed in the foundation. All this was intended to symbolize "the image of industrious, frugal and Christian France, the eternal France." On October 23, 1853 the casket was set into a cornerstone in the presence of the bishop and many important figures. Construction of the church was completed in 1855.

On October 7, 1944, at about two o'clock in the afternoon, the church at Baccarat was destroyed by the Allied air force because a German spotter was believed to be hiding in the belfry. The priest in his confessional, his penitents and a nun were killed in the blast.

In 1951, reconstruction of the building was begun. In clearing the ground, the magnificent weight with its thousand sparkling colors was found intact in its lead case. It was put on display at the Baccarat museum.

In 1858 paperweights in commemoration of the Maréchal Canrobert's visit to Baccarat were manufactured. One of these weights is now on display at the

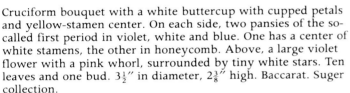

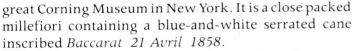

Cruciform bouquet with a white buttercup with cupped petals and yellow-stamen center. On each side, two pansies of the so-called first period in violet, white and blue. One has a center of white stamens, the other in honeycomb. Above, a large violet flower with a pink whorl, surrounded by tiny white stars. Ten leaves and one bud. $3\frac{1}{2}''$ in diameter, $2\frac{3}{8}''$ high. Baccarat. Suger collection.

Flat bouquet composed of a pansy, a blue and white primrose, a yellow wheatflower and a ''thousand petal'' rose in the center. Eleven leaves and two buds: a pink one on the right and a blue one on the left. Twenty-four-pointed star cut on the base. 3'' in diameter, 2'' high. One of a pair; the second weight is almost the same. Baccarat. Suger collection.

great Corning Museum in New York. It is a close packed millefiori containing a blue-and-white serrated cane inscribed *Baccarat 21 Avril 1858*.

Saint Louis also honored one of its directors, Eugène Didierjean, by creating a paperweight with the initials *E D* and *Saint-Louis 1867* for him. It was amber and decorated with a Legion of Honor medal encircled by a laurel wreath. Similar examples can be seen at the Musée de la Légion d'Honneur in Paris.

Baccarat catalogues refer to pansy weights up until 1907. Rock weights from the same firm are assumed to be from about 1880; lizard and salamander weights produced by Saint Louis could have originated at about the same time.

The Paris Exhibition of 1878 brought about a kind

of paperweight revival. Weights from the Pantin factory—on which unfortunately information is lacking —are dated from this period.

Paperweights were rarely signed and dated since they were fanciful objects which were considered more charming than valuable in their time. Identification is not always easy. Through examination of these mysterious crystal balls, careful connoisseurs, collectors, art historians and appraisers have managed to detect certain distinctive characteristics of a given factory. These identifications have been confirmed by spectroscopic analyses of glass and crystal composition done recently at the Corning Museum. In the next three chapters we will examine some of these characteristics more closely.

BACCARAT

In 1764 Antoine Renaut installed the first ovens of the Sainte Anne glassworks in Baccarat, under letters of patent delivered by the parliament of Metz to Monsignor Montmorency of Laval. The firm managed to last until 1816, when it was repurchased by Aimé-Gabriel d'Artigues, director of the Vonèche glassworks near Liège. French up until that time, Vonèche became Dutch territory after the treaties of 1815. Its output, which flowed mainly into France, was encumbered with customs duties. M. d'Artigues sold Vonèche and bought the Baccarat glass factory for 2,771 ounces of pure gold. In 1822, Baccarat was the foremost French glassworks and after the demise of the Creusot factory it produced the most beautiful crystal in the world; the heaviest (because of its 32% lead content), the most refractive and the most luminous. In 1843 it assumed the name *Compagnie des Verreries et Cristalleries de Baccarat* and in 1881 its current title: *Compagnie des Cristalleries de Baccarat*.

"Because of its [Baccarat's] predominance which was due both to the quality of its crystal and its high output, it did not seek to solicit customers by manufacturing fantasy objects and novelties such as paperweights. . . . As soon as a new product was successful, however, Baccarat would jump in and place products of superior quality on the market" (Y. Amic and R. Imbert, *op. cit.*). Its millefiori testify to "a perfection of technique which would remain unsurpassed."

Its paperweights, made of a clear crystal, are smooth, round, and barely flattened on the bottom. There are no striations or faults, no joints or swells around the base.

They can be distinguished by their lively colors, the precise designs in millefiori and by specific motifs in the so-called subject weights. The quality of the cutting should also be noted.

In all cases, the marriage of gay colors and glittering crystal gives Baccarat weights their characteristic coolness. Baccarat uses a richly colored palette—vermilion, royal blue, emerald green and lemon yellow.

In cross-section, the canes show fine, sharply defined silhouettes. Those which come up most often, and are thus the most recognizable, are:

trefoils or quatrefoils in red or green;

blue, green or red stars, often with a colored dot at the center;

tiny arrows, always pointed toward the center of the floret;

silhouettes in black, more rarely done in white or in colors.

Representative silhouettes are: a hunter with his gun; a red devil; and animals such as a rooster, deer, horse, dog, goat, elephant, butterfly, squirrel, pigeon, or pelican.

Their origin is as charming as it is unusual. A nine-year-old child, Joseph-Emile Gridel, passed time making paper cutouts of people and animals. His uncle happened to see them and decided to use the designs. He was Jean-Baptiste Toussaint, one of the directors of the glassworks. He had molds made of these twelve

Light green snake mottled with dark green. Dark pink eyes and nostrils. Set on a muslin ground. $3\frac{1}{8}$" in diameter. Baccarat. Suger collection.

Rock weight decorated by a forget-me-not. About 1880–1900. Baccarat. Private collection.

cutouts, whose motifs decorate many Baccarat millefiori. They are called "Gridel canes" and are an unmistakable signature.

Later, the child prodigy was associated with Gustave Courbet and became a painter of hunting scenes. His canvases were accepted for the Salon of 1865. His hunting expertise earned him the title of Master of the Wolf Hunt in the Baccarat area, where he died in 1901.

Millefiori florets are often sprinkled on muslin grounds (also known as lace grounds) made up of segments of clear canes in which white filigree strands are set.

The millefiori may form a tuft, standing upright like a mushroom, its head made up of millefiori packed tightly together, either close millefiori or concentric circles of millefiori. At the top of the base and all around the periphery an air ring is decorated by a blue or occasionally a red torsade.

Launay's letter of December 22, 1847, which mentions some paperweights perfected by Baccarat which were attracting large orders, probably refers to this type of weight, often dated 1847 or 1848.

Subject weights—flowers and animals—were apparently introduced about 1848–1851. Flat flowers were used. The most common, which appeared in 1849, was the pansy—a romantic symbol quite in vogue at the time and above all very allusive; it was often used as a token of friendship. Also very common were clematis with striped petals in white, blue, red or violet, and red or blue primroses decorated with white.

The camomile is made up of small crescent-shaped hollow canes. It is either solid red or salmon; blue and yellow; or white and blue. These flowers appear individually, often with a bud, or gathered in flat bouquets of two, three or four usually different flowers. The stems are sometimes crossed like an X. In 1848 tricolor bouquets appeared.

In all cases the leaves are alike and recall the spear-shaped leaf of the rose. They are always set in harmonious symmetry and usually in the same pattern.

Some Baccarat bouquets command high prices. Rare and highly valued are the rose and the buttercup.

Two animals are characteristic of Baccarat: butterflies and snakes. The first butterflies appeared in 1851.

Soft colors, typical of Saint Louis, are found in these three concentric millefiori paperweights. On the upper right, a piedouche weight. The cushion of millefiori rests on a ground of white latticinio which is also very typical. The stars are less pointed than those of Baccarat. Saint Louis collection.

Concentric millefiori signed and dated *SL 1848*. On the right, the same weight seen from above. Date and signature on the lower right. The central motif displays the special characteristic of the canes which make it up: in the center, a white cross with red border and around it seven hollow absinthe green canes with eleven other hollow canes with red interiors and crimped white exteriors. The arrows and stars are more rounded than those of Baccarat. Saint Louis. Boisgirard.

[24]

Sulphide with cameo of Louis-Napoléon Bonaparte encircled by a ring of canes in light blue and absinthe green, characteristic colors of Saint Louis. 3″ in diameter. Boisgirard.

Newel post with muslin ground. A subtle well-spaced arrangement of canes. The overall effect is one of remarkable harmony of colors with pink and absinthe green predominant. Saint Louis collection.

Saint Louis macédoines or scrambled weights, a mix of various cane segments. The English and Americans started a legend about them. They call them ''end-of-day'' paperweights because they were made in the evening from fragments of various canes used throughout the day. These discarded pieces would be gathered up to decorate less valuable weights with a jumble of different colors; they were made rapidly. This story has not been verified. Here, we see a miniature and a magnum in easily recognizable Saint Louis colors. Saint Louis. Private collection.

The faceting on this crystal vase creates a wide range of sparkling effects which are increased by the complex interplay of Saint Louis colors in the macédoine (scrambled) paperweight base. Saint Louis collection.

They have dark bodies and blue antennae. The four wings are made up of four florets lightly flattened to form ovals and to appear iridescent. Sometimes they are flitting around a flower, with a crown of florets on the periphery of the ground. This particular design is greatly admired.

The snakes—green, or brown flecked with green —lie on a muslin or rock ground. They are rare— understandably so, given their apparent low aesthetic appeal—and have a high commercial value.

Baccarat rock weights are perhaps more curious than beautiful. They enclose a formless mass of clay, sand and mica. Sometimes there is a flower; one containing a rose is known.

Collectors and American museums have ducks or swans swimming on a mirror ground simulating a pond. After a lengthy battle among experts, these rather unusual weights were finally attributed to Baccarat. Three of them may be seen at the Corning Museum, the greatest glass museum in the world. Another one may be seen at the paperweight museum at the Bergstrom Art Center in Neenah, Wisconsin.

Some weights have a base covered with two opaque layers—the bottom layer either red or blue, the top layer white. This top layer is engraved with the design of a horse in the same color as the bottom layer, in the middle of the white.

Similar in appearance are the paperweights bearing flat subjects enameled on gold leaf. The best known contain reproductions of the medal of the Legion of Honor. Three are known: one belongs to a French collector and is surrounded by florets; two are in the United States: the first bears the inscription *Bonaparte 1er, Consul 1802* and is now in the Corning Museum; the second bears the inscription *Napoléon 1er, roi des Français*. These weights are comparable to the sulphides, decorated with the silhouettes of royal, princely and imperial figures, which played a significant part

Wafer dish, flask in white filigree spirals, and colored crystal vase, on millefiori bases, two with macédoine design, the third with floating canes. Saint Louis collection.

Cut crystal flasks with millefiori bases whose motifs are repeated in the stoppers. Saint Louis collection.

< Variations on the close packed millefiori theme which are quite typical of Saint Louis: a piedouche, a doorknob and a cut crystal vase on a large paperweight base, signed and dated *SL 1845*. The light blue and ochre by the same firm dominate here. Saint Louis collection.

< Based on the idea of the scrambled weight base, three typical Saint Louis objects with other characteristics: filigreed torsade on the rim; engraved design; and at the right a white overlay. Saint Louis collection.

< A patriotic design in red, white and blue which inspired numerous paperweights is found in these related objects. On the left, the body of the small vase ($4\frac{7}{8}''$ high) is made up of two strands of filigree, one blue, the other white. The motif of the patterned millefiori base is repeated in the doorknob in the middle. At the right, a beautiful piece of glassmaking in the Venetian style, recreated by Saint Louis. Tricolor cane twists in opaque crystal ribbon, red on one side and blue on the other with white edging, alternate with white filigree or latticinio. They are flattened to form the top of the vase. In the crown base the strands are set in circular arcs. Saint Louis collection.

< Left, a wafer dish on a crown base with a concentric millefiori center. On the right, an elegant vase on a close packed millefiori base, signed and dated *SL 1846*; $7\frac{1}{8}''$ high.

(Detail of top weight, next page)

Cruciform millefiori design, four branches of white stardust canes with blue centers, each between two green and blue cane twists. Central motif in hollow blue and white canes and ribbed red canes with white sections. 3¼″ in diameter. Typical absinthe green and light blue are the dominant colors. Saint Louis. Suger collection.

in political propaganda favoring either the Empire, the Monarchy or the Republic, depending on the period.

Other enameled subjects are: Amour, springing from a rose; and a Greek lyre in bright red, blue and green enamel; these motifs also appear on other Baccarat pieces such as cut glass goblets.

Cutting is common in this firm's paperweights. All weights with a star cut base have been attributed to Baccarat. Although this is not always completely true, we can be sure that this factory, with its careful attention to detail, used refined cutting techniques and star cut the bases of its weights more often than its competitors did. Two other kinds of cutting have been noted: round windows and facets.

Round window cutting is done in two sizes:

large windows, six or seven on a single paperweight—one at the top, the others on the sides;

smaller windows—one at the top, seven to ten placed in two or three rows along the sides.

Facet cutting is seen on weights whose top was enlarged until its diameter was roughly the same as that of the base. The sides are cut in closely packed triangle or diamond shapes.

SIGNATURES AND DATES

Only a few millefiori weights from Baccarat are signed *B* and dated—only between 1846 and 1849—except for the weight discovered in the wall of the Baccarat church, dated 1853. Another millefiori at the Corning Museum is unusually marked *Baccarat 21 Avril 1858* on a large white star cane.

In the usual signature each character is molded in either red, blue or green on a small round white cane. A date inscribed on a small plaque indicates a fake. The canes are closely packed and a similar cane marked *B* is set over the two central numbers.

Alternating millefiori garlands, three with white canes with green centers and three with salmon canes with blue centers. Red stars and chartreuse canes at the center. Royal blue ground. 3⅛″ in diameter, 2″ high. Saint Louis. Suger collection.

SAINT LOUIS

The Saint Louis glassworks is located in the heart of the Moselle region of Lorraine, in the former county of Bitche. A glassworks had been established in the sixteenth century in the same place, amidst the beech and pine forests whose wood fueled their ovens. This factory was destroyed during the Thirty Years' War and was not to be rebuilt until Lorraine was returned to France in 1766. In 1767 Louis XV granted a charter to René-François Jolly et Cie. to build a factory using the name *Verrerie Royale de Saint-Louis*. It was there in 1781 that M. de Beaufort, the director of the enterprise, discovered the secret of making crystal, which up until that time had been made solely by the English. The Conseil d'Etat took it upon itself to protect this discovery; it forbade Saint Louis workers to leave the area without requesting leave two years in advance and forbade them to go more than a league away without permission.

At the Exhibitions of French Industry Products (held at the Champ-de-Mars and at the Louvre) of 1798, 1801 and 1802, Saint Louis met a competitor—the Creusot glassworks. At the 1806 exhibition, Creusot gained some ground. The quality of its products was improving; its crystal proved superior to that of Saint Louis. It was the most beautiful ever made in France, and contained even more lead than Baccarat crystal, which was manufactured later. Soon Vonèche in turn temporarily surpassed Saint Louis (1810), as much for the quality of its crystal as for its volume of production.

Saint Louis no longer participated in the exhibitions and seemed to retreat from the French scene. Its geographical location in the east of France led it to focus more on Switzerland and the German states than on the Parisian market. The factory thus came into contact with foreign styles and products such as those of Bohemia and Venice. This explains its mastery of decorative techniques related to coloring, whether transparent or opaque colors. Saint Louis was to master perfectly all filigree ornamentation. Its overlays and its rather complex cutting techniques also came to attract attention.

Starting in 1829 Saint Louis once again appeared at the Exhibition of French Industrial Finished Products, where it gradually began showing articles which heralded the paperweights to come: colored crystal, filigrees, opalines and other fantasy pieces in crystal.

Saint Louis seemed quite obviously suited to making paperweights. Furthermore, it used the same principle for all sorts of objects, such as desk sets and mantel ornaments as well as vases of all sizes. These items were mounted on paperweight bases. Saint Louis also made doorknobs or newel posts like millefiori balls or flower weights. Letters from Launay, the commercial correspondent in Paris, mention them as early as October 1848.

Characteristics of Saint Louis paperweights and related objects are: the softness of colors; the mastery of filigrees, especially visible in spiral latticinio grounds; and complex cutting which enhances optical effects and, in particular, magnifies the many small designs.

The crystal, containing 30% lead—a significantly higher proportion than the 24% required by international standards—is of high quality.

A garland of foliage with red, white, mustard and blue florets in a flatter-than-normal paperweight ($1\frac{1}{8}''$ high) next to a higher-than-usual weight ($2\frac{3}{8}''$) typical of Saint Louis butterfly weights. Saint Louis collection.

Red crystal wafer dishes. The one on the left is engraved with flowers which repeat the base garland of red, white and blue. On the right, a crown weight base. Both have white torsade rims. Saint Louis collection.

Paperweight containing flat red, white and blue flowers with millefiori centers. Only $1\frac{3}{8}$" high, $3\frac{1}{8}$" in diameter. Saint Louis. Suger collection.

Top and bottom: this millefiori mushroom encircled by a torsade of blue and white filigree represents a lovely combination of Saint Louis characteristics: soft colors, hollow canes, concentric arrangement, and torsade design in a stronger blue than Baccarat. $3\frac{1}{8}$" in diameter, $2\frac{1}{8}$" high. Suger collection.

Nosegay of five millefiori flowers placed on a lively muslin ground. Five spear-shaped leaves. Blue and salmon pink, the predominant colors in the bouquet, are taken up again in the border. Saint Louis. $3\frac{3}{8}$" in diameter, 2" high. Suger collection.

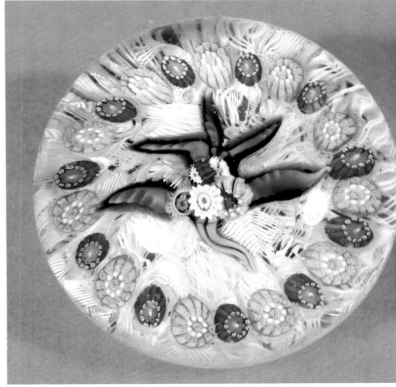

Among the extremely delicate colors are a very soft blue, pale ochre, absinthe green and lemon yellow. Blue seems to have been a dominant color in the first millefiori.

Motifs on a slice of millefiori cane recall those of Baccarat. They are, however, looser in design, in their stars and tiny arrows, for instance. The latter are arranged as if at random and are not turned toward the center of the floret. Three silhouettes appear: a dog, a dromedary and a charming pair of small dancing devils. Saint Louis has two-color square canes: round canes flattened with pincers. They are arranged in groups of four in either a square or diamond shape. The canes most characteristic of this company, however, are hollow rods. In most cases, they are light blue, smooth inside and tightly crimped outside. They may show two colors (white covered with red) or even three (white sandwiched between red and blue).

When they are gathered into an upright mushroom, the florets are carefully laid out in concentric circles and are rarely close packed. At the base, the ring around the foot of the mushroom is a filigree ribbon twisted about itself, while in Baccarat weights this torsade is made of a cylindrical rod with a filigree twisted around it.

The grounds are remarkable. Saint Louis is justly famous for the filigree which it cleverly fashioned into a basket pattern, still described by the Venetian word which indicates its origin—latticinio, from *latte* or milk. These filigrees are made of white opaque glass (known as milk glass), in this case crystal. This intertwining of filigree, with its wicker effect, seems to be composed of curved lines, indicating a spiral movement, hence the term spiral latticinio for these grounds.

Pink or blue jasper or sand cushions, flecked with white, are also a Saint Louis specialty.

Among Saint Louis subject weights, we find many flowers, as in Baccarat, yet on the other hand very few butterflies. The reptiles are lizards or salamanders, molded and fused on a hollow blown weight. While rare for Baccarat, fruits and vegetables are typical of Saint Louis, e.g. turnips and radishes.

Let us return to the subject of flowers. One is typical of the firm: the dahlia—pink or purple—either very small or completely filling the weight. The fuchsia is a specialty as well.

The camomile differs from that of Baccarat, with its heart of tiny arrows or stars. In Saint Louis the heart is made of very delicate yellow filigree stamens. We also find clematis with spear-shaped petals, striped with cobalt blue, pink and red.

The flat bouquets are small. Among the most beautiful Saint Louis creations are the upright bouquets—they are very small and often have a red, white and blue color scheme. A letter from Launay dated

< Vases mounted on paperweight bases with muslin grounds. Saint Louis muslin grounds are famous for their quality. At the center of the base on the left, a nosegay characteristic of Saint Louis. One vase has a white overlay, the other a blue. Saint Louis collection.

< Saint Louis has a predilection for small motifs which are magnified by the mass of crystal and by many small facets. Here is an example in this larger-than-normal paperweight containing a small flat nosegay with four florets and five leaves. Twenty-one facets cut on the top and eight windows on the sides; 3″ in diameter. Suger collection.

< Red clematis with ten veined petals with stem and five leaves around the flower. $2\frac{7}{8}$″ in diameter. Saint Louis. Boisgirard.

Superb vase with sides cut in a red flash overlay atop a muslin ground base, decorated by a large nosegay and a pink and absinthe green millefiori garland. Saint Louis collection.

[35]

October 30, 1848 assures us that the "fine bouquets," especially those with the white flower, were very popular. This same letter suggests cutting these paperweights and points out that "this is M. Lacloche's idea, who wants to see the effect this cutting will have before ordering newel posts with bouquets."

M. Lacloche was the proprietor of the boutique which was so famous at the time: l'Escalier de Cristal in the Palais-Royal, "where worldly people, the upper classes of society and rich foreigners went to see what rare and curious items French industry had to offer."

Saint Louis proved to be a master of cutting, and in styles more varied than those of Baccarat. The cutting of large round windows is similar to that favored by Baccarat. Its cutting of smaller windows uses smaller dimensions; three rows of small round windows may be observed on the side of the weight.

Facet cutting is typical and is done in such a way as to create optical effects.

There are two types of star cuts for the bases of these weights: small, with twenty-four narrow points for millefiori; and a larger, sixteen-pointed star for large flower or bouquet weights.

DATES AND SIGNATURES

Most Saint Louis weights are not signed. Some of their weights bear the initials *SL* and are dated from 1845 to 1849. The *S* is sometimes upside down.

CLICHY

Clichy, a mysterious but rather modest third factory whose files have disappeared, proved to be a formidable competitor for the two great glassworks in the area of paperweights. Launay warned Saint Louis on two occasions. A shipment of paperweights had contained too many articles of low quality. The Lorraine crystal factory lost the sale and as a result "Clichy cannot fulfill all the orders received." In 1849 Launay again complained that not enough attention was being focused on paperweights at Saint Louis, whereas Clichy had just lit a third oven to meet production demands.

Rouyer and Maës started the business in 1838 with the goal of manufacturing and exporting inexpensive items. The business seems to have taken off rather quickly and was transferred to Clichy at some point before 1844.

The new glassworks managed to take advantage of the crisis which had struck the larger older companies and had brought more affordable fantasy items into favor. Clichy also stressed the manufacture of paperweights; this was to contribute significantly to its prosperity.

At the Crystal Palace exhibition of 1851 in London Clichy displayed exquisite colored and overlay crystal, including some paperweights. In 1855 Clichy became the third-ranked French glassworks. In 1878, however, the company was sold and was incorporated into the Sèvres factory.

Strong colors, special patterns of millefiori canes and their arrangement in remarkably composed garlands, chequer patterns and concentric circles are some of the attributes which make Clichy weights so attractive. Some collectors consider them to be the most beautiful of all weights.

The material used then was a boracic glass which is very white and hard but lighter than crystal. Clichy weights weigh less than those of Saint Louis or Baccarat.

The glory of Clichy is its bright and rich colors. The intensity and the boldness of the juxtaposition of colors—working from a dark palette, with a characteristic violet, a deep emerald green and a vibrant red—make this firm's paperweights unusually beautiful.

This is all the more true because of Clichy's very unusual canes: pastry-mold canes, florets whose outer casing is deeply and clearly serrated; and spiral canes, hollow rods of different diameters one inside the other.

A veritable trademark of these weights is the most beautiful of all the millefiori florets, the Clichy rose. It is made up of overlapping curved opaline leaflets which are generally pink or white. A calyx of green with white interior (sometimes entirely white) surrounds the rose, as if to suggest leaves.

Finding a Clichy rose in a millefiori is a collector's delight. About one out of four Clichy paperweights have them. These roses may be in rarer colors—pale yellow, mauve, violet, deep wine red, pale blue, turquoise, and white with an outer row of red.

Other special characteristics of Clichy are its solid color grounds, consisting either of a vivid opaque ground, or a colored mass of transparent crystal—dark red, green, violet or cobalt; and its beautiful white muslin grounds.

Another Clichy trademark is the chequer pattern: each floret is framed by four pieces of twisted filigree, either white or in two colors ("barber pole")—white-and-blue, white-and-red or white-and-green.

Clichy has the only known moss grounds; they are very rare. They are created with very delicate short green canes set vertically between florets.

Clichy is in a class by itself as far as millefiori arrangement is concerned. This factory became famous for its garland patterns in various designs—all of them graceful and imaginative. Some are in the form of a *C* and are a kind of signature.

The high quality of upright millefiori mushrooms comes from Clichy's charming composition, which although apparently arbitrary is really quite elaborate. Less perfectly symmetrical than those of Saint Louis, their concentric design has an added note of elegant gracefulness.

A Clichy weight can often be recognized by its symmetrical and careful cane pattern when viewed upside down; note the parallel quality and the alternation of colors.

It is generally acknowledged that Clichy originated swirl weights, containing only canes of white, alternating with a color—pink, green, turquoise or blue—juxtaposed and curved to form a two-color

Beautiful white camomile with a center of delicate stamens. Encircled by four leaves and a bud set on a cushion of pink latticinio. $2\frac{1}{2}''$ in diameter, $1\frac{5}{8}''$ high. Saint Louis. Suger collection.

Pink pelargonium with five petals and five green sepals. Two spear-shaped leaves at the stem. The motif, quite small when seen flat from below, is enlarged more than twice by the crystal dome covering it. $2\frac{1}{2}''$ in diameter, $1\frac{5}{8}''$ high. Saint Louis. Suger collection.

Pelargonium with five blue petals separated by five green sepals, short stem with two leaves. Latticinio ground dear to Saint Louis. $3''$ in diameter, $1\frac{5}{8}''$ high. Suger collection.

Two flowers, each effectively a signature: a Baccarat pansy in a miniature weight—$1\frac{5}{8}''$ in diameter, $1\frac{1}{8}''$ high. On the left, a Saint Louis dahlia in a rare yellow color with stripes. Salmon and blue center. Five leaves. $2\frac{1}{4}''$ in diameter, $1\frac{5}{8}''$ high. Suger collection.

Purple dahlia with yellow and blue center and six green leaves. $2\frac{3}{4}''$ in diameter, $2\frac{1}{8}''$ high. About 1850. Saint Louis. Suger collection.

Pink camomile with four leaves and a bud. $2\frac{1}{2}''$ in diameter, $2''$ high. Saint Louis. Suger collection.

[39]

Pink camomile enclosed in a paperweight with a deep concave window hollowed out of the top and surrounded by a strand of the same color forming a snake. At the left, a butterfly—a rare piece of workmanship. Saint Louis collection.

Saint Louis arrived at subtle combinations with hollow canes. Here are two exceptionally rare examples. A double camomile in puff-ball shape with tiny center fills three-quarters of a crystal ball $3\frac{1}{8}$" in diameter and 2" high. On the right, a similar weight containing a group of hollow canes with green interiors around a millefiori center. Signed and dated *SL 1848*. $2\frac{3}{8}$" in diameter, $1\frac{1}{8}$" high. Saint Louis collection.

On a typical Saint Louis ground—blue and white jasper—a red clematis with three leaves and nine petals. At the center, a white cane with deeply serrated exterior. $2\frac{7}{8}''$ in diameter, $2''$ high. Saint Louis. Suger collection.

Delicate pink clematis in a careful and ordered design, with ten petals, yellow center and four leaves on spiral latticinio. Cut with eight round windows on top and six larger windows on the sides. Saint Louis. Suger collection.

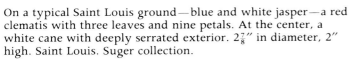

Three views of an upright bouquet of small flowers with base encircled by a torsade in blue and white filigree. Cut with seven round windows. $3\frac{3}{8}''$ in diameter, $2\frac{1}{2}''$ high. Saint Louis. Halphen-Meyer collection.

Upright bouquet encircled by a blue and white torsade. Extensive triangular cutting all over the surface. 2⅝″ in diameter, 2½″ high. Saint Louis. Suger collection.

Unusually shaped paperweight with large flat base decorated with twisted white filigree, the rim circled with a red and white torsade. The spherical knob encloses a small upright bouquet. Saint Louis collection.

Overlays are among the most valued weights. These are objects in clear crystal covered with layers of opaque crystal, which are then cut so that clear crystal reappears in certain places. Here is an exceptional overlay. It is cut with nineteen round windows which reveal an upright bouquet from various angles, thus multiplying refraction effects. The bouquet is encircled by a blue and white torsade. Musée de Saint Louis.

Seen from above, a Saint Louis turnip weight. A symmetrical composition with two white turnips, two mauve turnips and two radishes alternating regularly. Spiral latticinio ground. 2¾″ in diameter, 2⅜″ high. Suger collection.

[42]

swirl which visually fills the entire weight. Three-color swirls are known.

The swirl usually culminates in a floret at the top of the weight. This floret may be either a rose, large pastry-mold cane, or a motif made up of several florets grouped together in a circle.

Like Saint Louis, Clichy has some very pretty miniature scrambled weights, with green or blue being the predominant color. They resemble a well-tossed salad. A few are signed with a C.

The Corning Museum has a pair of superb vases, twelve inches high, all in macédoine (scrambled), with a few whole millefiori florets. Each is signed C L I C H Y on small individual canes.

Clichy concerned itself mainly with millefiori; therefore subject weights are rather rare. There are some very beautiful flat flowers—lily, convolvulus, gardenia and pansy—and flat bouquets which are rare and highly prized. Some upright bouquets can be recognized by their lively and beautiful colors: blue, navy blue and pink.

There are also overlays in marvelous strong colors which make them stand out: cobalt, deep red and dark emerald green.

Clichy did hardly any cutting on its paperweights; a few stars, some round windows and a diamond cut (a specialty) on the bottom of millefiori mushroom weights have been seen.

Clichy seldom signed its weights. One collector has a paperweight bearing the entire word Clichy; it may be unique. Some weights are known which contain a C signature cane.

REVIVAL

During their time, paperweights were in great demand, and not only by the vast public with limited means. Aristocrats and royalty were also interested in them. Empress Eugénie, Princess Murat and the Duke of Cardoza collected them. So did Empress Charlotte of Mexico, wife of the unfortunate Maximilian; this might account for the beautiful Mexican collections.

The collections of the royal court of England include paperweights which were probably collected by Queen Victoria; she went almost every day to the Great Exhibition of 1851 at the Crystal Palace. This exhibition marked Clichy's finest hour. It was the finest hour for paperweights in general as well. From this year on, Launay's correspondence no longer refers to paperweights. After 1855 written testimony, catalogues and exhibit summaries mentioning paperweights became rare both in France and Great Britain. In the United States, they had just come into vogue and were to remain popular until approximately 1880. Then, both in the United States and Europe, weights with inclusions became more and more sloppily executed. Designs gradually became less careful. They lost that certain balance in composition and attention to subtle detail which, when enhanced by technical perfection, made such fascinating objects.

Crystal balls, now more often being made of plain glass, ended up being a bazaar or flea market item. They sank to such a low level that even the masterpieces made during the classic period were seen in a bad light—even the first weights, perfected by artists from the three French factories.

The apathy towards paperweights was so great that the sources of these exceptional objects were forgotten. People were unaware that famous crystal paperweights had ever existed. Even the glassworks themselves were affected. They neglected this product so completely that they forgot its secrets. Records disappeared in the atmosphere of general indifference. Such was the total eclipse which would last for more than half a century.

Only a handful of nonconformists like the ill-fated English poet Oscar Wilde and French author Colette continued to collect paperweights. Colette was able to describe with great insight the guilt that certain women of the world felt in seeking out—even in the homes of concierges—these "delicious" balls: "It's probably a sin," says one of her characters in *Voyage égoïste*, in the chapter entitled *Paperweights*.

Mrs. Applewhaite-Abbott, a member of a powerful family of British glassmakers, tried to start a collection about 1900. Her husband was willing to allow "this weakness, provided they cost no more than five pounds apiece." When her daughter Lady Ruby Dugan wanted to give the most beautiful example of the collection to the Victoria and Albert Museum after her mother's death in 1938, she met with an indignant refusal.

Yet this Mrs. Applewhaite-Abbott, a pioneer in our eyes, had already made a convert of Mr. W. L. Way, who started his own collection in 1912. He wrote an article on the subject in 1920, the first to herald the revival of paperweights.

Saint Louis lizard or salamander paperweights draw on simpler techniques: the molded animal is set on the blown rather than molded weight. Here, a relatively harmonious example: a salamander in translucent topaz crystal on a clear crystal ball with gold decoration. $3\frac{1}{2}''$ in diameter. Halphen-Meyer collection.

Two weights which are typical, although miniature in size. Next to a classic Baccarat millefiori—signed and dated *B 1847*—$2\frac{1}{4}''$ in diameter, a common Saint Louis design: jasper ground, speckled with blue, green, pink and white. Here, the ground supports a large complex millefiori cane. Halphen-Meyer collection.

In Paris rare and valuable collections such as Jeanne Lanvin's were accumulating. In the work quoted above, published in 1928, Colette referred to a sale in Drouot the previous year where an unknown collector was breaking up his collection and people were bewildered by some of the bids.

A first-rate collector came on the scene: Zared Djevahirdjian. He bought his first paperweight, on his own initiative, in 1922 when he was barely thirteen years old. Thus began one of the most interesting collections in the world.

The real impulse, however, came from the United States, thanks to Mrs. Evangeline Hoysradt Bergstrom (1872–1958). Her collection was supposedly begun in 1917, but it was probably started sooner—perhaps in 1904, the year that her husband opened a paper mill in his home town of Neenah, Wisconsin. The couple moved there not long afterwards and lived there for the rest of their lives.

During an interview broadcast by a Chicago radio station in 1945, Mrs. Bergstrom related how she had become such an enthusiastic lover of paperweights:

Like many collectors—it all started from something my grandmother had and I enjoyed playing with as a child. That paperweight was of the millefiori type, I learned later, and it amused me by the hour to try to find two similar florets. Years later, in St. Petersburg, Florida, at an antique show, I found a weight like the one I loved as a child. It had a *B* with date *1847,* and the dealer told me the *B* stood for Bristol. I bought it after much deliberation, and also another which took my fancy. The first proved to be Baccarat, of course, and the second an American weight made in Fowlerton, Indiana, although I did not know it at the time. So I started with one French and one American and have been intrigued by them ever since, especially the French ones.

The Baccarat weight she describes is probably the number 2 listed in the Bergstrom museum catalogue— a millefiori with silhouettes—and the other weight is number 16.

As a matter of fact, Mr. Bergstrom, sensing the importance of his wife's collection, had the idea in 1951 of making a substantial bequest to Neenah for the building of a city museum. This bequest would begin upon the death of Mrs. Bergstrom. In 1953 she decided to include her home and grounds located on the shores of Lake Winnebago in the bequest. This became the seat of the Bergstrom Art Center and Museum which houses Mrs. Bergstrom's remarkable collection, and of a paperweight research center which is open to the

< Double overlay—blue on white—decorated with delicate gold leaf scrollwork. It is cut with six windows which reveal an upright mushroom. Star-cut base. Musée de Saint Louis.

< Very typical of Saint Louis and highly prized—its turnips (and radishes) on latticinio. Inside, there are two white turnips, two large red radishes, a violet turnip and a brown radish. $2\frac{7}{8}''$ in diameter. Boisgirard.

Crystal doorknobs treated as paperweights are especially characteristic of Saint Louis. Top, concentric millefiori with absinthe green the dominant color. On the left, a rare and beautiful motif—the fuchsia. In the center, two examples with pear and three cherries. Finally, a weight decorated with the famous nosegay. The last four weights on latticinio. Saint Louis collection.

< In a latticinio basket, a beautiful Saint Louis fruit composition: two pears, yellow and brown, and an apple alternate with three cherries and nine leaves. $3\frac{1}{2}''$ in diameter, $2\frac{1}{2}''$ high. Suger collection.

[47]

Below a classic Saint Louis close packed millefiori, an amazing creation by the same firm: two circles of segments of hollow cane, arranged on a slant, float in the clear crystal as if swept about in a whirlwind. $3\frac{1}{8}$" in diameter, 2" high. On the right, the precise arrangement in clear crystal gives the definite impression of suspension in the mass. The florets are actually arranged at the surface of an internal dome covered by a larger dome and sealed invisibly. The rose at the lower left indicates the origin of this newel post: Clichy. Saint Louis collection.

A rarity: a signed Clichy millefiori. It encloses one of the characteristic roses, near the center, and two turquoise and white florets encircling a red *C*, one at the bottom, one on the upper left. $2\frac{1}{2}$" in diameter, $1\frac{1}{2}$" high. Suger collection.

public—anyone can bring a paperweight to be identified. This is the only museum in the world devoted solely to paperweights. It is located about 150 miles north of Chicago.

Mrs. Bergstrom's work was not limited to this contribution alone. In 1940 she published the first significant book on the subject: *Old Glass Paperweights*.

Since 1935 she had kept a file in which each piece was listed with date of purchase, probable origin and description. Since the earliest date recorded here was 1917, it was believed that her collection did not go back any earlier. Actually, some pieces were noted as previous purchases whose date was forgotten. Mrs. Bergstrom was unable to begin her file earlier; she explains why in letters to her cousin Joel:

John [her husband] is on the road much of the time trying to get orders to keep the mill running. It is running only two and three days a week during these dreadful days of depression.

There was hardly any question of hunting about for additions to her collection, no matter how inexpensive they were.

With FDR's New Deal legislation, prosperity returned to the United States and Mrs. Bergstrom's shopping expeditions could resume. Between 1935 and 1944 she acquired 165 paperweights at $50; 111 for between $50 and $100; 127 for between $100 and $200; 86 for $200 to $500; and 21 for over $500. The most costly ones were bought for $2,200 in May 1941: a Saint Louis vase mounted on a ball containing a small upright bouquet (first wrongly ascribed to Baccarat, for characteristics were poorly known at the time) and, in November 1943, a red overlay in the Bohemian mode —its origin is still uncertain, probably Nicholas Lutz for the Boston and Sandwich Glass Company or the New England Glass Company, and it was made between 1852 and 1888.

In October 1942 she bought two beautiful Clichy mushroom overlays—a green one for $1,450, the other in cobalt for $725. In January of the same year, a delightful pink overlay with millefiori garland from Baccarat was acquired for $960 and in November 1943 three odd pieces which have not been conclusively identified were bought for $1000 each.

One of these weights has raised quite a few difficulties in terms of identification; it is one of those weights with birds on a pond, three ducks in this case. Today, the experts are fairly certain that it must be a Baccarat weight.

Other signs of the revival appeared in the United States. A first-rate collector in Dallas, Arthur Kramer, began to buy weights in 1930. A distinguished dealer, Charles Woolsey Lyon, realized that there was a demand for these objects and began to collect them. He found French weights in South America.

In the United States, special periodicals began to publish articles on this subject, magazines like *Hobbies, Antiques, American Collector* and *House Beautiful*.

In 1938 paperweights were shown at an exhibition in Chicago, and lectures were given on the subject. The Chicago Art Institute acquired antique English, American and French examples.

It was after World War II that paperweights were finally accepted and recognized. In the interim, the movement continued to grow in the United States—Europe had other concerns at the time, alas!

In 1940 two decisive events occurred: the exhibition of 186 magnificent paperweights belonging to F. M. Sinclair of New York at the Columbia County Historical Society in Kinderhook, New York; and the publication of Mrs. Bergstrom's study.

An American commentator has noted that this study—based on careful observations kept on filing cards—allowed comparisons and cross-checks, and made some identifications which were later corrected but nevertheless paved the way for a new appreciation of paperweights.

In his New York boutique in 1941, Charles Woolsey Lyon housed a remarkable exhibit for the benefit of the British who had been so hard hit by the war. Antique French paperweights held a place of honor.

Three charming weights. Above, a close packed millefiori in deep colors. Five Clichy roses are scattered throughout. On the edge, one sees alternate canes of white and pink arranged in a strict parallel pattern to form a precise border. At the left, a typical Baccarat dated *1847* with silhouette canes and a red clover blossom. On the right, a patterned millefiori ("barber pole—chequer") with fragments of white filigree and blue twist threads. A magnificent Clichy rose is ensconced at its center. Darys collection.

The "stave baskets" of Clichy weights, carefully composed and regular in design, are made up of two-color canes. One color is always white. These canes are arranged in parallel to form a staved basket to hold the close packed millefiori. Halphen-Meyer collection.

Clichy sulphide over cobalt crystal containing a cameo of the Comte de Chambord. On a ground of the same color, a scattering of deeply serrated canes which are very characteristic of Clichy, called "pastry-mold." In the center, a pink and green rose. At the bottom right, a rare green, red and white barber pole ground for the Clichy pastry-mold canes. On the left, a Baccarat miniature with muslin ground. Stars marked with dots can be seen; one of them is surrounded by tiny arrows atop four red and four green canes. Darys collection.

Clichy may be identified by its numerous garlands of every kind. On the left, a weight with six different chains. $2\frac{3}{4}''$ in diameter. On the right, a garland of blue canes. $3''$ in diameter. Halphen-Meyer collection.

Clichy perfected the rare moss ground, made up of delicate green canes representing well-cut grass, in which two garlands intertwine here. In the center, the green, white and pink pastry-mold cane and blue canes echo the colors of the garlands and the ground. $3\frac{1}{8}''$ in diameter. Clichy. Private collection.

Among other things, Clichy is famous for the beauty of its chequer patterns. Pastry-mold canes are framed by segments of white filigree tube which enhance their deep colors. Here is a newel post with a rose at the center. Private collection.

Clichy, noted for its strong colors, also knows how to work with paler shades. This newel post with a predominance of white and pale pink proves this perfectly. There is a white rose at the center. Five others are set in the framed spaces between filigree. There are four more with white petals and green sepals. Suger collection.

This is a rare and exceptional example with opaque green ground and exquisite panelling, around a magnificent center of sixteen roses, encircling eight canes in a strong characteristic green. $3\frac{1}{8}''$ in diameter. Clichy. Private collection.

Detail of a Clichy chequer patterned
millefiori with rose in the center.
The pastry-mold flowers are
in characteristic Clichy
shades: strong violet,
ultramarine, pink and
vivid light red.
Halphen-Meyer
collection.

Five garlands, each a different color, are placed on a muslin ground, encircling a large central rose. $2\frac{5}{8}''$ in diameter, $2\frac{1}{8}''$ high. Clichy. Suger collection.

Six garlands in a *C* shape enclose three rings of millefiori around a blue cane. Nearly translucent muslin
ground. 2¾″ in diameter, 1½″ high. Clichy. Suger collection.

Opaque color grounds are not rare for Clichy. On the left, the red ground reveals the special shape of Clichy canes. 2″ in diameter, 1½″ high. Suger collection.

The use of clusters or panels is also a characteristic of Clichy. This example shows four groups of similar canes, eleven green, twelve pink, ten white with green and yellow centers, and fifteen white with pink centers. Cobalt blue ground. 2¾″ in diameter, 1¾″ high. Suger collection.

This unusual paperweight marked with a large C is cut with numerous triangular facets which multiply the images of the canes making panels of eight circles, two of each color. Characteristic ground in strictly parallel latticinio tubes. 2⅞″ in diameter, 2″ high. Clichy. Suger collection.

Top left, canes in two circles around a pastry-mold cane in characteristic violet on a bright turquoise ground. A pink and green rose embellishes the smaller circle, a white and pink rose the larger circle. On the right, in a cobalt-colored crystal weight, two garlands intertwine. These two are by Clichy. Below, an amber flash base from Saint Louis enhances a small nosegay whose image is multiplied by complex cutting: seven large round windows on the sides, one on the top, seven smaller windows on the upper rim. Private collection.

Left, a miniature Saint Louis macédoine weight. Clichy created a specialty: two-tone swirls, with one spiral always white, the other green, mauve, pink or blue. On the right, an example 2⅝″ in diameter. Halphen-Meyer collection.

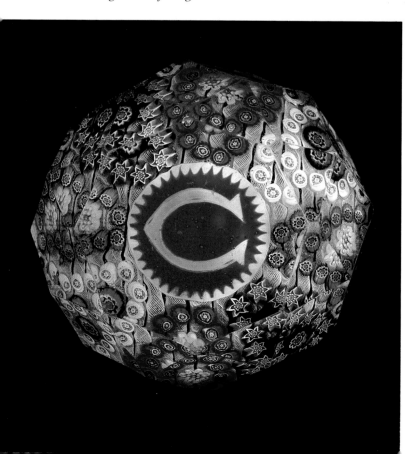

Newel post with millefiori, including at least four all-white roses, suspended in a clear crystal ball covered
with a high dome of the same crystal. Beside it, an unusual paperweight with *C* and *L* superimposed, encircled
by a ring of ten pink roses and one white rose. Clichy. Private collection.

Two beautiful Clichy swirl weights. One has a rose in the center, the other an ultramarine cane with pink center scalloped with white on the edges with a star in the middle. 3⅛" in diameter. Private collection.

It is largely thanks to Mrs. Bergstrom that differentiations among French, English and American items could be established. Enthusiasts in the United States, encouraged by her book, began to note these differences (especially in the French weights) and began or continued collections with greater confidence.

It was in Paris, however, in their place of origin, that French paperweights were to come back into their own, shortly after the war. In 1948 Mme. Yolande Amic, conservator of the Musée des Arts Décoratifs and M. Roger Imbert, specialist in the styles of the first half of the nineteenth century, published *Les Presse-Papiers Français de Cristal* (which is unfortunately out of print). This work sometimes comes up at auction among the very items to which it is devoted, and its price is understandably quite high.

Collections began to crop up all over the world and prices climbed briskly. In Egypt, Farouk (the future King) fell in love with French paperweights and was ready to buy everything in one fell swoop at certain sales. When he was deposed in 1952 he left a collection which was so large that it weakened the market when it was dispersed.

In Argentina, Eva Duarte Perón added a paperweight collection to her riches. In the United States, novelist Truman Capote was caught up in the fever. A French importer of Saint Louis paperweights, Paul Jokelson, discovered old French paperweights in 1923 and would soon start the Paperweight Collectors' Association, which publishes an extremely interesting annual bulletin.

Mr. Amory Houghton, whose family headed the powerful Corning Glass Works in America, served as ambassador to France from 1957 to 1961. He took advantage of this stay to put together a very beautiful collection which he brought back to the United States. It may be seen at the Corning Museum of Glass. Corning publishes an annual summary of in-depth studies on glass *objets d'art—The Journal of Glass Studies—*and has a first-class museum of glass products. Corning is a small town in New York State, located approximately 300 miles northwest of New York City.

In 1978 the Corning Museum organized a superb exhibition of paperweights (the majority of them

Very rare four-leaf clover. It is enclosed here in a 2¾" high, 3⅛" wide ball which makes it seem larger than it really is. The inclusion seems to be about 2" high but is really only ¾" high. Clichy. Private collection.

Flowers and facets: from left to right, a bottle stopper containing a flat blue-white-red bouquet; a newel post enclosing an upright bouquet in the same colors, encircled by a torsade in blue and white; and a seal also decorated with a tricolor upright bouquet. All three are from Saint Louis. Beautiful Clichy newel post with many concentric canes and all over faceting. Private collection.

French) by combining loans from collectors with its own collection. It was held from April 29 to October 21 and offered the public a complete panorama of the subject. Its catalogue is quite authoritative. The title is borrowed from a sixteenth-century Venetian phrase: *Paperweights: "Flowers which clothe the meadows."*

The United States, therefore, has the two richest and most interesting museums exhibiting paperweights. There are nineteen other museums displaying these objects, such as the New York Historical Society, which received the exquisite Sinclair collection as a bequest. The Art Institute of Chicago must be added to this list. It was blessed with a large, high-quality collection: 1,200 pieces donated by Arthur Rubloff, the most important of all collectors. His gift has been appraised at about four million dollars. He had become the greatest collector in the world upon the death in 1959 of Colonel Robert Guggenheim of Washington, D.C. On assignment at the Embassy in Lisbon in 1940, the Colonel had begun a valuable collection which ultimately contained 600 pieces.

Mr. Rubloff was triumphant in a famous sale in London in 1966. Through Howard Phillips, an antique dealer specializing in glass, he acquired a lovely Clichy flat bouquet with the rare convolvulus for the sum of £5,200 at Sotheby's. Until 1969, this was the highest price ever paid for a paperweight.

Later, important paperweight sales took place in London and New York through Sotheby's or Christie's. In Paris, however, two appraisers, Claude Boisgirard and Axel de Heeckeren, specialized in these articles and attempted to draw them to l'Hôtel Drouot.

Maurice Lindon of France bought Jeanne Lanvin's superior collection in 1939. Since that time, he has become famous for his meticulous requirements in choosing weights. He also was a hero in an adventure —that of the rare and unique yellow overlay from Saint Louis.

In 1945 an English antique dealer bought the weight for £200. In 1950 he sold it to Maurice Lindon for £500. Lindon then wrote an enthusiastic letter about the purchase to Mrs. Bergstrom, explaining that he had just become the lucky collector to find and acquire a yellow overlay. He pointed out that it resembled one shown in Mrs. Bergstrom's book—that he had a green one of the same type, that Palmer Hart had one in blue and Mrs. Bergstrom had one in blue and white. He added that he had also seen one in pink and white.

This letter is full of enthusiasm. Evelyn C. Cloak reprints it in her work which updates Mrs. Bergstrom's book, *Glass Paperweights of the Bergstrom Art Center.*

In 1957 M. Lindon sold this paperweight at Sotheby's. Mr. Amory Houghton bought it for £2,700, then donated it to the Corning Museum.

Here are some additional figures which give an idea of price developments:

Superb concentric millefiori with a remarkable combination of colors which change to darker shades from the center out. The center is composed of five pink roses around a small white rose. Extremely well-made stave basket of parallel blue and white canes. 3″ in diameter, 2″ high. Clichy. Suger collection.

Wonderful concentric millefiori suspended around seven roses encircling the center. Very elaborate cutting, which enhances this composition: large concave window at the top and three rows of twelve windows on the sides. $2\frac{3}{8}$″ in diameter, $2\frac{1}{8}$″ high. Clichy. Suger collection.

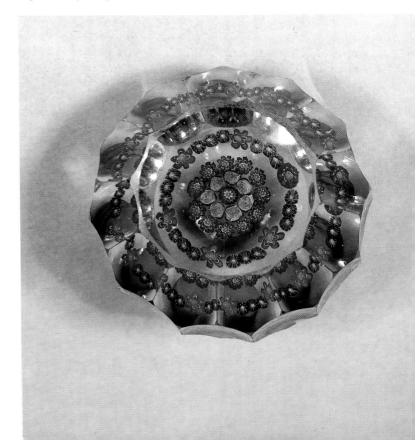

In weights which are somewhat lighter than the crystal ones from French firms, flowers evoke Saint Louis and Baccarat examples. Suger collection.

Five cherries, one of them white, on a branch with five large leaves. $3\frac{3}{8}''$ in diameter, $2''$ high. Approximately 1870–1880 (?). Unknown origin; probably from the Pantin factory. Suger collection.

Two weights also attributed to Pantin—one containing a fig on a stem with three leaves, the other bearing a strawberry and five leaves. The larger one—$2\frac{3}{4}''$ in diameter, $2''$ high—has a beautiful dome above the motif. Star-cut base. Strawberry is a miniature $1\frac{5}{8}''$ in diameter, $1\frac{1}{8}''$ high. Suger collection.

Rare nosegay from Clichy. It brings to mind Saint Louis patterns, but the colors and the shape of the canes leave no doubt as to the origin of this paperweight. Beautiful muslin ground on a bed of seven parallel latticinio canes. $3\frac{1}{8}''$ in diameter. Suger collection.

December 2, 1963: during the sale of the Maba collection, a red salamander weight from Saint Louis brought £3,800; a rare blue Baccarat flower, 9,000 francs;

July 3, 1967: at the sale by Manuel Gonzalès de Cosio, an engineer in Mexico City, a pink overlay from Saint Louis went for $9,500;

May 10, 1968: a red salamander weight, 46,600 fr.;

July 3: the same weight brought 72,000 fr.;

September 3: a green snake weight from Baccarat, 25,000 fr.; a Saint Louis overlay, 44,000 fr.;

October 28: a superb turquoise overlay with close packed millefiori from Clichy, 9,849 fr.; and a flat bouquet in red, white and blue from Baccarat, 18,000 fr.;

January 27, 1969: one of the famous ducks on a pond, Baccarat, reached 71,500 fr.;

March 17: a Clichy, 32,500 fr.;

October 30: a Baccarat made prices skyrocket by bringing 88,400 fr.;

January 26, 1970: a Baccarat, 40,000 fr.;

March 16: a Clichy weight broke a record at 110,500 fr.;

1979: an unusual Saint Louis encased gingham overlay brought $117,600 at Christie's;

and in December 1983 at Sotheby's of New York, a rare Pantin silkworm weight from the collection of Paul Jokelson sold for $143,000.

These spectacular figures apply only to extremely rare pieces which are not always remarkable weights from an aesthetic point of view. Interesting, quality paperweights of undeniable charm remain accessible at far lower prices.

One guess is that approximately 50,000 paperweights were made during the classic period by the three great French glassworks, half of them by Baccarat. About 20,000 may have survived. Many disappeared or were destroyed during the period when they fell into disfavor. They were given to children as playthings.

The two great French glassworks, Baccarat and Saint Louis, made an effort to recover processes which had been lying dormant, when faced with the revival of antique paperweights. The decisive moment came in 1951 for Baccarat with the chance discovery of the 1853 millefiori in the foundation of the church which was then being rebuilt. After long and careful work, re-creations of classic paperweights have been released and other designs have been produced as well, all of them inspired by weights more than a century old.

Thus the revival of old techniques has been complemented by fresh new ideas; and it seems that glass paperweights will be with us forever.